Dr Susan Musikanth is a counselling psychologist. Her areas of research and interest are stress, depression and interpersonal relationships. She also works as a human resource consultant conducting stress and depression management workshops for helping professionals (doctors, social workers, etc.), businessmen and women, education-alists and the general public. Susan has recently completed a book on depression and paints on canvas in her spare time. She lives with her family in Cape Town.

STRESS MATTERS

SUSAN MUSIKANTH

WILLIAM WATERMAN PUBLICATIONS

The names and circumstances of individuals in illustrative cases have been changed to protect their identities.

Published in 1996 by William Waterman Publications
A division of William Waterman Publications (Pty) Ltd
PO Box 5091, Rivonia 2128

First edition, first impression 1996

ISBN 1-874959-32-3

Book Design: Iskova Image Setting
Typesetting and Reproduction: Iskova Image Setting
(in 11 on 13 point Bookman Light)
Cover design and illustration: Crazy Cat Design Studio
Printed and bound by: Colorgraphic, Durban

Is Stress a dirty word for you?

Learn to minimise stress as danger and
maximise it as opportunity for excellence.

An easy-to-use programme to follow,
at your own pace, in your own time.

Dedicated to my late parents
Sonny and Diana Hirsch

and

to my sons
Evan and Paul Musikanth

with deep gratitude and love

CONTENTS

FOREWORD

That Sue Musikanth is an expert in dealing with stress is best illustrated by the compliment she extended to me in asking me to write this foreword knowing that I was close to being a workaholic and that, until I read and applied *Stress Matters* (what a beautiful catch 22!), my time management was bad with consequent impact on the delivery of my small contribution to this valuable book. I am probably the ideal person to write this foreword in that the only way I managed to remain within limits when I added up my scores in the stress questionnaire contained herein was the accident of simultaneously being teetotal, not smoking and having recently given up coffee.

Joking aside, in *Stress Matters* Sue Musikanth has done a marvellous job of identifying, in a simple manner for the lay person, many of the real pressures both, insidious and patent, of modern living. She has also given readers the comfort of knowing that these are neither incurable nor peculiar, and has given practical advice to enable the reader to activate and adopt responses, which not only neutralise the negative effects of each pressure, but convert them into positive forces in their everyday lives.

Obviously the greatest benefit will be derived from attending a stress-management workshop and using *Stress Matters* as a home tutorial to reinforce the practical experience of the workshop. However, for those not fortunate enough to be able to enjoy this experience, the text is straightforward and easy to apply and the reader will enjoy most of the benefits of a workshop if only he, or she, uses some of the time-management techniques suggested to make time for application of the remedies suggested.

I have no hesitation in recommending this book to everyone. Those who already cope with and use stress to an advantage will better understand why they have been able to do so, and will do better in future, and most of all, those who are not coping will learn to accept and use stress so as to enhance their lives. Congratulations to Sue Musikanth for succeeding in one of the most difficult tasks and that is, as an expert in a complex field, being able to outline both the problems and solutions in terms which can be fully understood by the lay person while at the same time providing food for thought for the expert.

Prof. John R P Morris
Cape Town
CA(SA) ACMA
Tax consultant and
member of the Tax Advisory Committee.

ACKNOWLEDGE- MENTS

To Elka Arelisky for typing my workshop into organised form.

To Adele Rifkin for typing the first draft of this book.

To Kerry Abramowitz for the first editing of this book.

To BJ and Jonnie for letting me cut my workshop teeth on your company.

To Paul Tomes and Melanie Green of Business Presentation Skills for fine-tuning this programme.

To Prof. John Morris for a fund of helpful information regarding stress and business. Also for your encouragement to write this book and for agreeing to write the foreword.

To Irene Berman for your creative ideas and useful criticisms − and your delicious friendship.

To Cheryl Salkinder for listening to my ideas and for unconditional friendship.

To David Shoolman for inspiring the wonderful cartoons of OG.

To Jill Levett for your invaluable information on stressors of executive partners.

To my clients and delegates for the privilege of sharing your lives with me and for the mutual learning that has issued from these interactions.

To Prof. Kevin and the late Patricia Atkinson for teaching me about the value of making art a stress manager and for friendship.

To Annelie Nortje for being there right at the beginning.

To Connie Valkin for sharing your exquisite articulations and for being my Johannesburg connection.

To Hilary Zelter for being there for me — even at such long distance.

To Neville Serman for your encouragement, caring and support.

To Ester Richards of Exclusive Books for guiding me in the right publication direction.

To Jacqui Greenop of William Waterman Publications for your expert final editing of this book.

INTRODUCTION

This book has been designed and presented as a practical workshop for you to work through on your own. For this reason it is necessary for you to have certain materials on hand.

You may purchase the Stress Kit (order form is at the back of this book). The kit comprises:

○ a jotter;
○ modelling clay/plasticine; and
○ an audio-casette: deep-muscle relaxation with creative visualisation and music.

You may also purchase the relaxation cassette on its own.

You will in addition need to obtain:

○ a variety of coloured felt-tipped pens;
○ a few old magazines;
○ glue;
○ some of your favourite music; and
○ an audio-casette player/recorder.

If you do not wish to purchase the Stress Kit, you will need:

○ a few coloured felt-tipped pens;
○ some old magazines;
○ glue;
○ some of your favourite music;
○ modelling clay/plasticine;

- ○ an audio-cassette player/recorder; and
- ○ an unlined jotter which you will find at the back of this book.

Hold a small piece of modelling clay in your hands (from your kit or purchase modelling clay/plasticine from your local stationers).

Switch on your favourite music.

Take a few deep breaths.

Close your eyes and visualise how you feel in terms of stress at the moment and how you would like to feel in the future. Do not think.

Allow it to happen.

Get in touch with the music and with the feel of the clay. Open your eyes.

Model the clay.

Do not try to model anything in particular. You will be surprised at what you have created.

Many stressed people model cubes or boxes — a way to contain and control themselves and their worlds.

A paint salesman, at one of our workshops, modelled a woman's figure — seemingly asleep. He was unwilling to share the interpretation of his model. He told me after the workshop that his wife had recently died.

A young student modelled a beautiful rose that was half opened. She explained that she was frightened to expose her thoughts and feelings in her environment, but felt the potential to spread her petals as her confidence grew.

Quite a few people model balls or interlocking circles. They talk of wholeness (the balls) and/or interaction between different dimensions of their lives (work, home, parents).

We frequently find our participants stretching the clay to breaking point. They describe how they are so stressed that they feel as if they are going to snap.

2

It is interesting how our subconscious mind comes to the fore and what we are able to understand about ourselves through our creations.

Learning to manage stress through creativity is one of the strongest cornerstones of this workshop.

Life without stress is, at best, boring and, at worst, dead. When this truism is accepted, the stresses of modern man are harnessed and maximised for peak performance and excellence.

Life with stressors that are too many, too frequent, too prolonged or badly managed is known to result in symptoms that range from chronic headaches to heart attacks, work absenteeism, accident-proneness, reduced job performance, stress burnout syndrome, exhaustion, depression and anxiety.

This programme aims to inform you about:

- ○ stress ;
- ○ its causes;
- ○ differing perceptions of stress; and
- ○ a multifaceted and effective approach to managing stress.

The above information will be complemented with the practical application of deep-muscle relaxation and certain aspects of assertiveness training: refusal of unreasonable requests, effective handling of criticism and negotiation of workable compromise. We started this programme with clay modelling and shall end it with making a collage – to concretise what you have learned from the workshop and what you will take with you to use in your life.

In essence, this programme will demonstrate that a lifestyle balanced by a variety of optimally stimulating stressors/ challenges, together with 'slow down' periods, bodes well for a healthy, satisfying and productive existence.

The clay modelling that you created earlier helped you describe yourself qualitatively in terms of stress. It is also important to assess your quantitative level of stress. To this end, please complete the stress questionnaire below and total up your score.

STRESS QUESTIONNAIRE

Answer the following questions to establish your level of stress. Choose one statement that best describes your response to each question.

1. Your partner's or colleague's behaviour upsets you. Do you:

   (a) Explode?

   (b) Feel angry but suppress it?

   (c) Feel upset, but do not get angry?

   (d) Cry?

   (e) None of the above?

2. You have a huge pile of work to get through in one morning. Do you:

   (a) Work very hard and complete the lot?

   (b) Leave the work and look for other ways to pass the time?

   (c) Complete what is within your capability?

   (d) Prioritise the load and complete only the important tasks?

   (e) Ask someone to help you?

3. A friend makes some unkind remarks about you in conversation with someone else. You happen to overhear. Do you:

   (a) Interrupt the conversation and tell the person exactly what you think of them?

   (b) Walk straight past and forget about the incident?

   (c) Walk straight past, but start thinking about revenge?

   (d) Walk straight past and think about the person?

4. You are stuck in heavy traffic. Do you:

(a) Hoot?

(b) Try to take another route to avoid the congestion?

(c) Switch on the radio or cassette?

(d) Sit back and try to relax?

(e) Sit back and feel angry?

(f) Do some work?

(g) You do not have a car so you would not be in a position to make these choices.

5. When you play a sport, do you play to win

(a) Always?

(b) Most of the time ?

(c) Sometimes?

(d) Never. You play for enjoyment?

6. When you play a game with children do you deliberately let them win?

(a) Never.

(b) Sometimes.

(c) Most of the time.

(d) Always.

7. A deadline is looming, but you are not satisfied with the work you have done. Do you:

(a) Work on it all hours to ensure perfection?

(b) Panic because you think you will miss the deadline?

(c) Do your best in the time available without worrying about it?

8. Someone tidies up your house/office and never puts things where you left them. Do you:

   (a) Mark the position of everything and ask the person to put your things in the places you have indicated?

   (b) Move everything back into place once the person has left?

   (c) Leave most things as they are — the occasional change does not bother you?

9. A close friend asks you for your opinion about a room that has just been decorated. Do you:

   (a) Think it's terrible and admit this?

   (b) Think it's terrible, but say otherwise?

   (c) Think it's terrible, but only discuss the aspects that you like?

   (d) Think it's terrible and offer suggestions on how to make it better?

10. When you do something, do you:

    (a) Always try to produce something perfect?

    (b) Do your best and not worry about achieving perfection?

    (c) Think that everything you do is perfect?

11. Your family complains that you spend too little time with them because of work. Do you:

    (a) Worry, but feel that you have no control over the situation?

    (b) Take work home so that you can be with them?

    (c) Take on more work?

    (d) Find that your family has never complained?

    (e) Reorganise your work so that you can be with them more?

12. How would you describe an ideal evening?

    (a) A large and swinging party?

    (b) Doing something with your partner that you both enjoy?

    (c) Escaping the rat race by yourself?

    (d) Dinner with a small group of friends?

    (e) A family evening doing things that you all enjoy?

    (f) Working?

13. Which of the following do you do?

    (a) Bite your nails?

    (b) Feel constantly tired?

    (c) Feel breathless without having been physically active?

    (d) Drum your fingers?

    (e) Sweat for no apparent reason?

    (f) Fidget?

    (g) Gesticulate?

    (h) None of the above?

14. Which of the following do you suffer from?

    (a) Headaches?

    (b) Muscle tenseness?

    (c) Constipation?

    (d) Diarrhoea?

    (e) Loss of appetite?

    (f) Increase in appetite?

    (g) None of the above?

15. Have you experienced one or more of the following recently (the last 3-4 weeks)?

   (a) Crying or wanting to cry?

   (b) Difficulty in concentration?

   (c) Forgetting what you were going to say next?

   (d) Irritation over trivialities?

   (e) Difficulty in making decisions?

   (f) Wanting to scream?

   (g) Feeling that you have no one with whom you can really discuss things?

   (h) Feeling that you are jumping from task to task without really completing anything?

   (i) Have not experienced any of the above?

16. Have you experienced any of the following during the last year?

   (a) A serious illness (yourself or someone close to you)?

   (b) Family problems?

   (c) Financial problems?

   (d) None of the above?

17. How many cigarettes do you smoke a day?

   (a) None?

   (b) One to ten?

   (c) Eleven to twenty?

   (d) Twenty-one or more?

18. How much alcohol do you consume in a day?
    (a) None?
    (b) One or two drinks?
    (c) Three to five drinks?
    (d) Six or more drinks?

19. How many cups of coffee (not decaffeinated) do you drink a day?
    (a) None?
    (b) One or two cups?
    (c) Three to five cups?
    (d) Six or more cups?

20. How old are you?
    (a) 18 or below?
    (b) 19 – 25?
    (c) 26 – 39?
    (d) 40 – 65?
    (e) 65 or over?

21. You have a very important appointment at 9.30 in the morning. Do you:
    (a) Have a sleepless night worrying about it?
    (b) Sleep very well and wake up reasonably relaxed, but thinking about the appointment?
    (c) Sleep well and wake up looking forward to the appointment?

22. Someone close to you has died. Naturally you are very upset. Do you:

    (a) Grieve because no one can ever fill that terrible gap?

    (b) Grieve because life is so unfair?

    (c) Accept what has happened and try to get on with your life?

23. You have got into trouble over a problem. Do you:

    (a) Assess the situation on your own and try to find another solution?

    (b) Discuss the problem with your partner or close friend and try and work something out together?

    (c) Deny that there is a problem in the hope that it will go away?

    (d) Worry about it but make no attempt to try and solve it?

24. When did you last smile?

    (a) Today?

    (b) Yesterday?

    (c) Last week?

    (d) Cannot remember?

25. When did you last compliment or praise someone in your family or at work?

    (a) Today?

    (b) Yesterday?

    (c) Last week?

    (d) Cannot remember?

SCORES

Add up your score for each question

1. a = 0   b = 0   c = 3   d = 0   e = 1
2. a = 1   b = 0   c = 1   d = 3   e = 2
3. a = 0   b = 3   c = 0   d = 1
4. a = 0   b = 0   c = 2   d = 3   e = 0   f = 2   g = 1
5. a = 0   b = 1   c = 2   d = 3
6. a = 0   b = 1   c = 2   d = 3
7. a = 0   b = 0   c = 3
8. a = 0   b = 0   c = 3
9. a = 0   b = 0   c = 3   d = 1
10. a = 0   b = 3   c = 0
11. a = 0   b = 0   c = 0   d = 0   e = 3
12. a = 1   b = 3   c = 0   d = 1   e = 2   f = 0
13. a = 0   b = 0   c = 0   d = 0   e = 0   f = 0   g = 0
     h = 1
14. a = 0   b = 0   c = 0   d = 0   e = 0   f = 0   g = 0
15. a = 0   b = 0   c = 0   d = 0   e = 0   f = 0   g = 0
     h = 0   i = 1
16. a = 0   b = 0   c = 0   d = 2
17. a = 3   b = 1   c = 0   d = 0
18. a = 3   b = 2   c = 1   d = 0
19. a = 3   b = 2   c = 1   d = 0
20. a = 3   b = 0   c = 1   d = 2   e = 3
21. a = 0   b = 1   c = 3
22. a = 0   b = 0   c = 3
23. a = 2   b = 3   c = 0   d = 0
24. a = 3   b = 2   c = 1   d = 0
25. a = 3   b = 2   c = 1   d = 0

YOUR SCORE

51 – 68 Your stress level is low. You show very few signs of stress. You are not a workaholic. You thus show Type B behaviour and generally cope very well with stress.

33 – 50 Your stress level is moderate. You show some stress. You are not a workaholic, but there is some tendency towards it. You therefore show mild Type A behaviour and generally do not cope well with stress.

16 – 32 Your stress level is high. You show many signs of stress. It is likely that you are a workaholic. You thus display Type A behaviour and do not handle stress very well.

0 – 15 Your stress level is very high. You show a great deal of stress. You are a workaholic. You display extreme Type A behaviour and your ability to deal with stress is very poor.

Adapted from Looker & Gregson (Assess your Stress) in *Stresswise*.

1

WHAT IS STRESS?

Please turn to a blank page in the notepad from your kit. If you do not have a kit, take a blank piece of paper. Take a pen or pencil and head the page:

Physical Stresses

Jot down a list of all the physical symptoms of stress that you have experienced or are presently experiencing, for example headaches, stomachaches.

Take another sheet of blank paper and head it:

Emotional Stresses

Write down all of the emotional/psychological signs of stress that you have or are aware of, for example anxiety, depression.

Eustress and Distress

Stress may be viewed as positive or negative. Positive stress is termed 'eustress' and negative stress is termed 'distress'.

The table overleaf highlights the differences in 'eustress' and 'distress' by comparing the physical and emotional characteristics of each.

COMPARISON OF THE PHYSICAL CHARACTERISTICS OF 'EUSTRESS' AND 'DISTRESS'	
Eustress	**Distress**
Physical fitness	Unfit
Increased energy	Fatigue
Improved concentration	Poor concentration
Efficient memory	Poor memory
Healthy libido	Low libido
Calm and relaxed	Muscular tension
Healthy eating patterns	Overeating/loss of appetite
Good sleeping habits	Insomnia
Good health	Awareness of heartbeat
	Palpitations
	Cardiac problems
	Breathlessness
	Dry mouth
	'Butterflies' in stomach
	Increased cholesterol
	Indigestion
	High blood pressure
	Nausea
	Headaches
	Constipation
	Diarrhoea
	Accident proneness
	Muscular aches and pains
	Frequent viruses

Eustress	Distress
	Sweaty palms
Moderate consumption of alcohol/drugs/cigarettes	Increased consumption of alcohol/drugs/cigarettes

COMPARISON OF THE EMOTIONAL CHARACTERISTICS OF 'EUSTRESS' AND 'DISTRESS'	
Eustress	Distress
Winning	Losing
Succeeding	Failing
Being euphoric	Feeling depressed
Achieving	Failing to achieve
Feeling stimulated	Feeling bored
Assuming responsibility	Failing to take responsibility
Feeling excited	Feeling disillusioned
Feeling confident	Lacking in confidence
Having good self-esteem	Having poor self-esteem
Being empathic	Being self-involved
Being sociable	Being anti-social
Being assertive	Not being assertive
Feeling happy	Feeling unhappy
Being flexible	Being inflexible
Being creative	Showing lack of creativity
Being tolerant	Being critical
Being effective	Being ineffective

Eustress	Distress
Having good time management	Having poor time management
Being efficient	Being inefficient
Being rational	Being irrational
Being decisive	Being indecisive
Being productive	Being under-productive
Having a sense of humour	Lacking a sense of humour
Being in control	Being out of control
Being clear thinking	Having confused thinking
Being positive	Being negative
Being relaxed	Being anxious/irritable
Not worrying	Worrying
Being active	Being passive
Being motivated	Being unmotivated

Whether stress is good (eustress) or bad (distress) in terms of its effect on one's physical and emotional functioning – it can best be described as **the way in which the body and mind respond to threats and demands from the environment**.

The Life Event Questionnaire opposite should now be completed to assess stressful changes and pressures from the environment – and the risk of these to your health.

LIFE EVENTS

Check your score of events over the past year:

Death of partner	100
Divorce	73
Separation from partner	65
Jail sentence	63
Death of close family member	63
Injury or illness to yourself	53
Marriage — your own	50
Retrenchment	47
Reconciliation with partner	45
Retirement	45
Ill health in member of family	44
Pregnancy — your own	40
Sexual problems/difficulties	39
Addition of new family member	39
Major business or work changes	39
Change in your financial state	38
Death of friend	37
Change to a different type of work	36
More arguments with partner	35
Take on a large mortgage	31
Mortgage or loan foreclosed	30
Change in responsibilities at work	29
Child leaves home	29
Trouble with in-laws	29
Outstanding personal achievement	28
Spouse begins or stops work	26
Child begins or ends school	26
Change in living conditions	25
Change in personal habits	24

Trouble with boss or employer	23
Change in working hours or conditions	20
Change in residence	20
Child changes schools	20
Change in religious activities	19
Change in social activities	18
Change in sleeping habits	16
Change in number of family get-togethers	15
Change in eating habits	15
Holiday	13
Religious holiday	12
Minor violations of the law	11

Adapted from Holmes & Rahe's 'Life Change Index'.

Holmes and Rahe suggest that a score of over 100 points puts you at risk of a stress-related illness during the next two years. My opinion is that a score of over 200 points is dangerous to your health.

Og the Caveman

One concrete way to demonstrate the body's response to stress is to imagine Og the caveman, who could be one of your ancestors.

Og goes hunting for food. He sees a dinosaur approaching. He is terrified in the face of this danger. Og's muscles tense in response to the fear. Danger signals reach the base of his brain — more specifically, the hypothalamus. The hypothalamus releases chemicals to the pituitary gland. The pituitary gland in turn sends more chemicals and hormones to the adrenal glands, above the kidneys. The adrenal glands release adrenaline and noradrenaline into the bloodstream and to all the body functions. The body is then finely tuned to the 'fight or flight' response. Og fights the dinosaur or he runs away from it. He has thus burnt up the chemicals and hormones and subsequently calms down.

In primitive times, humans used their muscles to ward off danger.

Agricultural Og

In agricultural times, people worked off their stresses in the fields. As long as the farmer of today is 'hands on' and not a 'city farmer', he or she also works off the chemicals and hormones in day-to-day work on the farm. You often hear of the physically exhausted but relaxed farmer who heads home at the end of a day.

Industrial Og

During the Industrial Age and amongst our present day 'blue collar' workers, a day was and is characterised by a great deal of physical activity. Whilst these workers have not had the benefit of outdoor activity in nature, they certainly burnt up/burn up harmful stress chemicals and hormones.

Modern-day Og

In modern times, people are at times faced with life-threatening events where it is appropriate to fight the danger or to run away from it.

In general, however, modern people are faced with different stressors and pressures, threats and demands than those faced by our ancestors.

Turn to an empty page in your notebook. Head this page: *My Stressors*. Write down all of the pressures and stressors that face you in your day-to-day living.

2

GENERAL STRESSORS OF MODERN TIMES

Here is a list of modern-day general stressors that have been found to impact on physical and emotional functioning:

- violence;
- threat or opportunity of change;
- unpredictability;
- financial pressure;
- work overload;
- time pressure;
- ongoing responsibility for others;
- family demands on time;
- criticism at home and at work;
- life event changes such as death or divorce;
- lack of religious/spiritual direction;
- marital or relationship discord;
- traffic jams;
- change due to technology;
- excessive noise;
- excessive materialistic values; and
- lack of privacy.

In addition to those listed above, there are certain stressors relating to particular groups of people.

Helping Professionals

The people that fit into this category are medical doctors, dentists, psychologists, social workers, physiotherapists, nursing sisters, occupational therapists and speech therapists. Helping professionals are regularly subjected to the following stressors:

- never being 'off duty';
- daily contact with unhappy, sick or injured people;
- unrelenting responsibility for others;
- pressures of satisfying conflicting demands of patients, colleagues and family relationships;
- pressures of a full waiting room;
- long hours;
- ethical dilemmas;
- shouldering the patient's emotional problems;
- difficulty in refusing patients' unreasonable demands on time;
- staff problems; and
- lack of privacy.

Case Study

Dr Smith, a 35-year-old general practitioner, consulted with me, complaining of fatigue and lack of motivation, irritability with his patients' 'trivial' complaints, conflicts with his elderly partners' old-fashioned medical practices and high levels of stress related to his wife's nagging for more of his time. He was suffering from regular, severe headaches and heart palpitations.

His patients do not hesitate to call him out at night and over weekends — often for symptoms that could have waited for normal surgery hours. Doctor Smith reported that he had no time for golf, which had been his 'passion'.

He felt guilty about taking time off from his wife and two young children for sport. He also felt inadequate in that he believed that doctors should not suffer from symptoms of stress or depression.

Educationalists

University and college lecturers, school and college principals and teachers, remedial teachers and educational psychologists would be classified under this group. Typical stressors that affect them are:

○ criticism by parents;

○ daily demands of students;

○ ongoing responsibility to cater for the varying needs of many students;

○ interstaff 'politics';

○ balancing home life with work; and

○ after-hours demand for work.

Case Study

Dorothy Kussen is a 41-year-old mathematics teacher at a private high school. She had been widowed at 35, with two pre-adolescent sons. Her husband had not provided well in terms of life assurance and Dorothy was struggling to support herself and her sons. She attended one of our workshops for teachers where she described dizzy spells and nausea. She was exceptionally tired and felt each day to be a trial. It was a month prior to the final exams when she fainted at school and was rushed to hospital. Her blood pressure and cholesterol were dangerously high. Her doctor had suggested that she attend one of our workshops.

Dorothy reported that she was under so much pressure at school and at home that she could no longer cope. She could not,

29

however, afford to either stop working or parenting. She was a perfectionist who needed to extract one hundred and fifty per cent from each of her pupils. The principal and parents of her pupils were, in addition, constantly demanding more from her in respect of time and effort. Her sons were now of an age where fashion and socialising were priorities in their lives. They expected new and expensive clothes, entertainment money and as they were growing boys, consumed the contents of the fridge almost before she had the opportunity to unpack the groceries.

Dorothy felt guilty at not giving sufficient time to her pupils and excessively guilty at not being able to provide a comfortable living for her sons. She was at the same time angry at her late husband for having deserted the family by dying and for not having had the foresight to leave them financially more comfortable.

Her parents were elderly, and they criticised her for not spending enough time with them and for neglecting their grandsons. Dorothy had no time for socialising as she was coaching mathematics after hours to supplement her income. She had also gained thirty kilograms in weight over the past two years as she ate junk food due to lack of time to prepare and eat properly.

Professionals in Business

The term 'professionals in business' embraces attorneys, accountants, architects, pharmacists, engineers, computer scientists and journalists. Stressors that they encounter on a daily basis are:

○ conflicting demands on time by clients and family;
○ long hours;
○ criticism by colleagues/clients;
○ pressure deadlines;
○ ethical dilemmas;
○ taking personal responsibility for the clients' problems; and
○ inability to refuse clients' unreasonable demands on time.

CASE STUDY

Jane Harper is a 40-year-old partner in a busy legal practice. Her speciality is family practice, including divorce. She is married with three teenage daughters.

Jane had been referred by her doctor to a stress management workshop for attorneys. She was presenting with symptoms of 'stress burnout syndrome'.

Her previously good sexual relationship with her husband, a businessman, had dwindled to once every few months, which created tensions and arguments in the marriage. Jane complained that she had recently lost weight, was constantly tired, but could not sleep. Once she fell asleep she would wake up and constantly re-run trials in her head. She would agonise about tense negotiations between her clients and their spouses as well as the latter's attorneys and advocates. She had nightmares about her ever-increasing workload and the pressures from her partners to consult and bill more clients. She regularly screamed at her children for demanding more of her time.

Businessmen and Businesswomen

Entrepreneurs, executives and managers fall into this category. Their stressors are:

○ long hours;
○ full responsibility for staff performance;
○ full responsibility for the financial wellbeing of the business;
○ threat of economic and political change and uncertainty;
○ strain of frequent travel;
○ juggling of time between work and home;
○ workaholicism; and
○ heavy traffic.

31

CASE STUDY

Geoffrey Davis was a 42-year-old owner of a successful second-hand car business. He travelled frequently, both locally and overseas. He had been divorced for six years and had had several long and short-term relationships — none of which could be sustained.

Geoffrey's ex-wife succeeded in making him feel guilty for his financial success, for travelling and spending time away from his children. On his return from trips, she would run him down to his children (whom he adored) and refuse him access to them unless he regularly increased her maintenance payments, bought her new cars and every sort of luxury for the children.

In addition, his ex-wife had managed to sabotage any relationship that he had had. Geoffrey attended a workshop held for businessmen and women. He reported the above problems, as well as the fact that he felt betrayed by his sales staff who were stealing from him, and in whom he had placed great trust.

He found it difficult to make time for himself. Geoffrey felt guilty that he had achieved substantial financial rewards in his business and was therefore unable to join in the laments of his peers about financial pressure. Most people he knew were jealous of his success. In addition, many women who had became involved with him made it clear that the most appealing thing about him was the security that his financial position could offer them. This made him wary and almost paranoid in his interactions with strangers. At the same time he longed for a settled lifestyle with a caring, loving partner.

Executive Partner

Spouses and partners of executives are also subjected to regular stressors. These are:

○ time pressures;

○ lack of space;

○ inability to say no to unreasonable demands;

- responsibility for running the home and bringing up the children (if there are any);
- no tangible reward for highly responsible duties;
- no recognisable status in their own right;
- little time for personal development/career;
- demands of partner's practical and emotional needs;
- need to be a perfect partner;
- need to be an untiring, listening ear;
- need to be well-groomed and 'on show' for all social/ business occasions;
- demands of frequent and excellent home entertainment;
- need to be seen as strong and coping at all times;
- must not become sick or depressed;
- must have good knowledge of partner's company, be politically correct and have a good general knowledge for dinner or conference conversation;
- must take care of partner's physical and emotional health;
- must serve as mentor and role model for other executive and management partners;
- must not have a different opinion in public to that of their partner;
- must always remember the names of business colleagues and staff.

CASE STUDY

Lora Mallett, 50 years old, an attractive, robust woman, told me that she was struggling to get up in the mornings. Married to John, the director of a large clothing manufacturing company she had always been a highly efficient wife and mother to her five children. She was now feeling tired and anxious and afraid of being seen as a failure. 'Everyone depends on me for everything. I am exhausted, but neither my husband nor my children understand how much responsibility I carry on my shoulders. I am no longer as young or energetic as I used to be.

'John has now reached the top of his field. While he was climbing the ladder and being stimulated and entertained at lavish breakfasts, I was knee high in nappies, nursery and primary schools and the boring conversations of other mothers. I am now doing the balancing act of business entertainment with menopausal symptoms: hot flushes, weight gain, memory loss and the feeling that I am not as attractive or sexy as I used to be.

'The children are getting on with their lives. All of a sudden John and I are left in a rambling house without anything to say to each other except about the time or place of our next dinner or the place of the next conference or if I could take his suit to the dry cleaners. I am so bored. I have to develop friendships during the day as we do not have time for normal socialising as a couple.

'Our children complain to me that they can never find the right time to ask their father's advice on important career or personal matters. He is always too busy, preoccupied, away on business or exhausted. They find him emotionally absent, even when he's at home.

'John and I travel locally or internationally at least twice a month. I need to be a supportive companion to him as well as perfect, smiling, well-groomed and knowledgeable about the company and about business associates that we are meeting. At the same time, I must make sure that my grown-up children's practical and emotional needs are satisfied. The children are super but *so* demanding. I have had to postpone a hysterectomy for eighteen months to fit in with John's hectic schedule.

'I used to walk with my friends and do pottery. It helped me to cope better but I no longer have the time or energy to do these things anymore. I don't know how to make more time in my life. I am feeling anxious and depressed and crying more often (but only in private). My life feels aimless without a sense of purpose and no real satisfaction or achievement. My days are filled with nebulous activities like hunting for clothes to fit my ever-increasing frame. What a frustrating and stressful life, when all I want to do is to stop and smell the roses and do something constructive for me for a change. I want to feel my worth.'

Single Working Mother

Single working mothers are regularly exposed to the following stressors:

- ○ financial pressure;
- ○ responsibility for the children's emotional wellbeing;
- ○ diminished status in the eyes of society;
- ○ loneliness;
- ○ tiredness from working and catering to the children's needs;
- ○ guilt at not having a 'complete' family;
- ○ very little space and time alone;
- ○ pressure of working when babies or small children are ill;
- ○ stressors of starting and continuing relationships between demands and jealousy of children and pressures of work;
- ○ inability to refuse manipulative requests of children due to need to compensate for lack of father; and
- ○ ongoing conflict with ex-husband.

CASE STUDY

Rosemary MacMillan, a 25-year-old divorced mother of a toddler and small baby was divorced and lived in a small one-bedroomed apartment. Her husband had had an affair and left Rosemary for the 'other' woman when the former was six months pregnant with their second child. He paid very little maintenance and made no effort to see the children.

Rosemary had moved to South Africa from the United Kingdom as a young, single woman seeking adventure. It was here that she had met her husband, had fallen pregnant and had been pressured by his family to marry.

Rosemary worked as a teller in a bank. She had been called in by the personnel officer who told her that there had been complaints that her till was not balancing at the end of the day. Also, she had been reported by clients as being rude, abrasive and unhelpful.

Rosemary consulted with me individually. She became tearful and told me that she was under financial pressure, that both of her children had been ill with chickenpox and had kept her up at night. She was no longer invited out by friends from her marriage — they excluded her as she was not a 'couple'. Her girlfriends feared that she may pursue their husbands.

She was perpetually exhausted as when she was not at work, she was attending to the demands of her children, who were frequently whining or crying. Even though she had not sought the divorce, she felt that she had somehow failed as a wife, as her husband had found someone more desirable than her. She also felt inadequate in not providing a 'complete' family for her children.

Rosemary had been invited on several dates that she cancelled at the last minute when her toddler became insecure and clinging as she was readying herself to go out.

To add to her stresses, her ex-husband would telephone on a regular basis to point out that she was ill-equipped as a mother and unstable as a person and would make threats of fighting her for custody of the children, despite the fact that he saw little of them and was unreliable with maintenance. Rosemary seriously considered suicide as a way out.

Single Working Father

Single working fathers also encounter stressors in their day-to-day lives. These are mainly:

- loneliness;
- stress of 'losing' the day-to-day family activity;
- guilt at depriving the children of their father;
- inability to refuse unreasonable requests of the children;
- pressure of providing financially for two households;
- conflicting demands of a new relationship and those of his children on his time;
- jealousy by children of new girlfriend/wife or partner's children;

○ sense of failure; and
○ ongoing conflict with ex-wife;

Case Study

Don Gordon, a 53-year-old divorced father of four teenage children was an accountant and had been living on his own for the past year. He attended one of our workshops, where he explained that, during the last year, he had contracted 'flu viruses and bronchitis on five occasions. He never felt well. His ex-wife, who had never worked, had left him as she had found their life boring. Don had worked hard to build a successful business and had managed to pay off their large home in a prestigious suburb.

His ex-wife succeeded in securing a large cash settlement, as well as a car and the total proceeds of their home and all the furniture for herself.

He now found that he had to borrow from the bank to make a new home. Besides losing a substantial amount of money to his ex-wife, Don found that his biggest loss was that of day-to-day contact with his children. Although he was a hard worker, he had always been a hands-on father to his children.

Whilst the financial loss made him angry and resentful, it was the loss of daily contact with his children that broke his heart.

He found that he was trying to compensate his children by giving in to their excessive financial demands. Don had met and become seriously involved with a woman.

This had added extra pressure in that his and her three teenage children made every possible effort to sabotage their relationship by displays of jealousy and had refused to attend social or family gatherings where Don and his girlfriend were present.

Besides the frequent viruses, Don suffered from severe headaches that rendered him incapable of work.

He frequently argued with his girlfriend as she had complained of the minimal time available for her. His clients demanded his constant attention and the exceptional service that they had been used to. He no longer had the time or inclination to give attention to them due to his other pressures.

Modern-day Og

Modern-day Og's body reacts to these pressures and demands in precisely the same way as Og, the caveman, did.

The problem is that Modern-day Og does not use the 'fight or flight' response to burn up the chemicals and hormones. The modern human's body is on the alert for action — aroused and stimulated over a prolonged period of time. In this situation, physical and emotional systems experience wear and tear, harm and illness.

3

DIFFERING
PERCEPTIONS OF
STRESS

The stressors described in the previous chapter of the individual and of different groups of individuals clearly impact on physical and emotional processes. It is, however, the individual's perception of these stressors that translates them into harmful stressors or challenges.

Chinese wisdom is evident in its depiction of 'crisis' as a combination of 'danger' and 'opportunity'.

Take the case of the housewife who resorts to tranquillizers when the housekeeper takes her annual holiday. A single, working mother uses that opportunity to involve the family in household duties that draw them closer to one another.

Consider two affluent business executives who face bankruptcy in recessionary times. The one suffers debilitating depression and anxiety and may even consider suicide. The other, although deeply distressed, uses the opportunity to re-evaluate priorities and values, scales down the family's standard of living and eventually finds great joy in the small things in life, with more time for the family and greater spiritual involvement. Gail Sheehy* wrote of the high sense

---

* Sheehy, G. *Pathfinders*

of wellbeing of people in her study. These people tend to face adversity as challenges where they use creativity and risk-taking to overcome work and home crises.

A further example is the physical or mental health professional (doctor, psychologist, social worker) who, through therapy, actually harms the patient. In therapy, when faced with their error, the one professional will deny responsibility for the actions taken, become angry and defensive and blame the patient and the system for the harm caused. The other professional will assess the situation carefully, take responsibility for the mistake and grow and learn from the experience.

It appears then that some people crumble emotionally and become physically ill when faced with events they perceive as crises. Others tap the depths of their emotional and physical resources to maximise life's challenges.

4

OPTIMAL LEVELS OF STRESS

Some people clearly perceive and manage stress more effectively than others. There are times, however, when the best stress managers are overtaxed with too many, too frequent or too prolonged demands that threaten their sense of being in control, and that may lead to 'stress burn-out syndrome'.

Case Study

Susan Pringle, a 35-year-old married woman with a 7-month-old baby, is Managing Director of a medium-size printing and publishing company. She attended one of our stress-management seminars and complained that she was feeling depressed and tearful, with constant fatigue and anxiety.

She explained that prior to the birth of her baby she had excelled in her job, had substantial salary increases from her chairman and managed to balance the many and varied demands of work with a good home life that included rest and relaxation.

With the birth of her baby, she had found that she could not cope with the excessive demands that now faced her. Her husband had become resentful of the time she spent at work and with the baby

41

and had felt that he was not receiving sufficient time nor attention from her.

Because of this he was critical of her role as wife, mother and career woman. At the same time, he expected that she continue to earn a high salary so that their standard of living should not drop. He demanded this when she suggested that she look for part-time employment.

At the opposite end of the scale is the dull and uninteresting situation where too few stressors impinge on the individual's life. This is called the 'stress of boredom'.

Case Study

June Newton, a 45-year-old married woman with two adolescent children, had been until a year ago, the manager of a vast investment portfolio for a large bank. She had decided that she needed a career change and would first like to take a year off work to give her family and herself time to establish new, richer contacts.

Her husband, a self-confessed workaholic, had respected June when she was heavily involved in her work. She attended one of our seminars where she described herself as bored, tearful, clinging to her husband and demanding approval for her new role from him and her children. They had continued with their busy lives, where she had found that her confidence and self-esteem had reached rock bottom.

For peak performance and health, it is necessary to operate at an optimal level of stress. It is here that pressures and challenges fall within the person's realm of capability and where there is the capacity to learn new coping skills when faced with new crises and challenges.

The concept of peak performance is well illustrated by the *Yerkes-Dobson Law* — Effects of stress on performance and on health. *(Refer to the graph on the following page.)*

Individuals do not have control over the presence or frequency of many life events: the death of someone close, wars, the economy. It is how these are handled, however, that determines whether they will benefit or become destructive to the self and to others.

People do have the capacity to maximise and optimise performance. This is made possible by including new and different stressors into their lives (studying a new language, playing a competitive sport, learning to play a musical instrument). These should be balanced by periods of rest and relaxation (deep-muscle relaxation, non-competitive sport, communication with family and friends, listening to music, art appreciation or simply regular short trips into nature or into the garden).

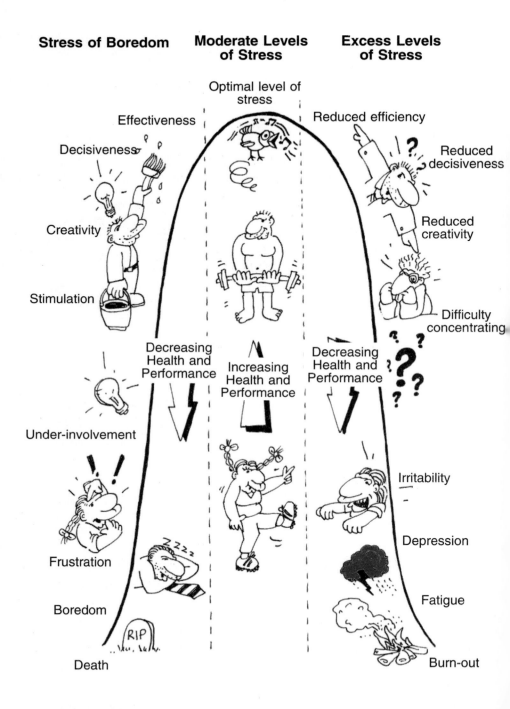

Stress of Boredom

Moderate Levels of Stress

Excess Levels of Stress

Optimal level of stress

Effectiveness

Decisiveness

Reduced efficiency

Reduced decisiveness

Creativity

Reduced creativity

Stimulation

Difficulty concentrating

Decreasing Health and Performance

Increasing Health and Performance

Decreasing Health and Performance

Under-involvement

Irritability

Depression

Frustration

Boredom

Fatigue

Death

Burn-out

Yerkes-Dobson Law — **Effects of stress on performance and on health**

5

STRESS-
MANAGEMENT
TECHNIQUES

Please turn to a blank page in your notepad. Head it:

Own Stress-Management Techniques

List your own techniques for stress management, both positive and negative. It will be helpful for you to retain those that are positive and intergrate them with the new methods and ideas from this programme.

One of the most effective methods of handling stress is deep-muscle relaxation with creative visualisation and music.

Deep-muscle Relaxation with Creative Visualisation and Music (Please listen to Side A of your audio-casette.)

If you do not have the kit, you may read the instructions (see following section headed 'Method for Deep-muscle Relaxation with Creative Visualisation and Music') on to a blank audio-casette and then play them back to yourself.

Effective stress management utilises left-brain functioning (the conscious, critical, analytic, logical and intellectual

45

faculties: studying a new language, problem-solving, learning to make art, learning to play a musical instrument).

There is also a focus on right-brain functioning (the subconscious, intuitive, perceptual and sensory faculties: listening to music, appreciating the beauty of nature, responding to intuition in making decisions).

Deep-muscle relaxation, one of the most effective and least time-consuming methods of stress management,will be used here with creative visualisation and music. During this exercise, the left brain, or conscious mind, will be put into 'neutral' or left to rest. The right brain, or subconscious mind, will be focused on and stimulated. Your only task will be to allow the power of your subconscious mind to control your body. The muscles will relax and the use of your senses (in creative visualisation) will further enhance your sense of relaxation.

Method for Deep-muscle Relaxation with Creative Visualisation and Music

Sit comfortably on your chair. Loosen any clothing that might be tight. You may change your position at any time and this will not disturb your sense of peace and calmness. You will be fully aware of my voice and any noises around you or outside this room. These will not disturb you. I am now going to ask you to system-atically tense and relax all the muscle systems in your body. If any of your muscles are injured or painful, do not tense these.

Tense your fists, as tight and hard as you can . . . bend your arms up to make your biceps tight . . . move your elbows towards each other so that you feel the muscles pulling across your back . . . suck your stomach in . . .

47

don't forget to breathe... press down with your heels and lift your toes up to tense the muscles in your legs... close your eyes tight, clench your teeth and press your lips together... bend your head backwards to make the muscles in the front of your neck tight... breathe through your nose...

Feel the tightness and tension right through your body...

Now let it go... take a deep breath and allow your muscles to relax... continue to breathe deeply and rythmically... each time you breathe in, feel yourself breathing in peacefulness... as you breathe out, feel tensions draining out of your body through imaginary holes at the bottom of your feet... keeping your eyes closed, I am once again going to ask you to tense the muscles as I name them and then release the tension to demonstrate the difference between a state of extreme physical stress and relaxed peacefulness...

Tense your fists, your biceps, your stomach, your legs, your eyes, your teeth, your jaws, your neck... now let them go... take a deep breath and let yourself relax deeper and deeper... let your breathing continue to be deep and rythmical...

As you sit there with your eyes closed, I am going to count backwards from three to one... as I do so you will feel yourself getting lighter and lighter until, at the count of one you open your eyes, let them close and allow yourself to go deeper and deeper and more relaxed than you are now... three... two... one... you can now open your eyes, let them close and go deeper, more peaceful and relaxed... your breathing deep and rythmical... each time you breathe in you breathe in calm and peace. As you breathe out, any tension left in your body flows out the bottom of your feet.

Sitting calm, relaxed and peaceful, I want you to imagine a place or scene that you have visited where you have felt completely relaxed. If you have not experienced such a place, make one up ... put yourself into that scene in your mind and get in touch with all the sensations you associate with it ... see the colours and shapes that are there... feel the textures that surround you ... feel the temperature... hear the sounds ... smell the odours ... and taste the tastes ... take a deep breath and breathe those sensations of peacefulness into your body and go deeper ... peaceful, calm and relaxed ... your breathing is deep and rythmical ...

I am once again going to count backwards from three to one suggesting lightness with each count ... you may find that your subconscious mind wishes you to go deeper and deeper with my counting rather than lighter and lighter ... it does not matter which, but at the count of one you will open your eyes, allow them to close and go deeper than you are now ...

Three ... two ... one ... open your eyes, let them close and go deeper ... peaceful and relaxed ... I now want you to imagine there is a soothing liquid inside your head ... let it be a colour and a temperature that you find to be relaxing ... let the liquid move inside your head ... slowly, gently massaging the muscles ... leaving them limp, heavy and relaxed ... feel the liquid move into your neck ... soothing, healing and relaxing the muscles ... into your shoulders ... dissolving any tensions that might still be there ... into your arms relaxing the muscles and leaving them heavy and limp ... into your back muscles ... massaging, healing and soothing ... into your chest ... relaxing the muscles and leaving them heavy ... into your sto-mach ... massaging and relaxing the muscles ... into your hips and pelvic area, relaxing and soothing the muscles ... into your legs, dissolving any tensions that might still be there ... feel the liquid flow into your feet,

49

massaging the muscles and releasing tensions... now feel the liquid flow out through the imaginary holes at the bottom of your feet... take a deep breath and as you breathe out go deeper... peaceful, calm and relaxed...

I am now going to count backwards slowly from five to one... suggesting lightness as I do so. Whether you go deeper and deeper or lighter and lighter with my counting will depend on the wishes of your subconscious mind... at the count of one you will be able to open your eyes; you will feel refreshed as if you have had a long holiday... you will feel alert but with a deep sense of peace and inner confidence... you will know the power that your mind has over your body... five... four... three... two... one... you can open your eyes.

Relaxation occurs faster and deeper the second time you practise the technique. It follows, then, that the more frequently the method is practised, the less time it takes to achieve deep-muscle relaxation and the more efficient and effective it will be.

Also, the use of techniques from your own experience will provide a personalised combination that is well balanced, varied and particularly suited to your own lifestyle. It may, for example, be useful to play music cassettes in the car for the stress of heavy traffic. You may choose to relax at home in a warm bath (with or without music) or to go out into the garden and relax in nature, again with or without music.

Now let your eyes close... concentrate on your breathing and you will find that with each breath out you relax deeper and deeper... count backwards from three to one a few times... each time you reach one, open your eyes... let them close and become more fully relaxed than before... three... two... one... open your eyes... let them close and relax deeper... three... two... one... open your eyes... let them close and go deeper... with your mind and body relaxed, feel the soothing liquid flow through your body, take yourself in your mind to your peaceful scene... hear the music and watch the reflected patterns the light makes on your eyes... feel the effects of the music broadening and enriching your sense of calm.

Slowly count backwards from five to one... you will gradually feel yourself going lighter and lighter... or deeper and deeper... whichever your subconscious mind decides... at the count of one you will be able to open your eyes feeling refreshed, peaceful, calm, and relaxed... five... four... three... two... one... open your eyes.

Steps to Deep-muscle Relaxation

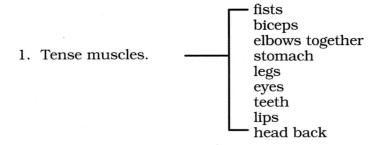

1. Tense muscles.
   - fists
   - biceps
   - elbows together
   - stomach
   - legs
   - eyes
   - teeth
   - lips
   - head back

2. Relax muscles.

3. Deep breathing.

4. Counting backwards from three to one.

5. Special place — breathe in sensations.

6. Counting backwards from three to one.

7. Liquid.

8. Counting backwards from five to one.

Additional Methods of Harnessing and Maximising Stress

This programme emphasises the importance of learning a broad and varied repertoire of stress-management techniques. These may be used singly or in combination, when appropriate to particular circumstances, at any given time.

To this end, further stress managers are considered below. These have been accumulated from our professional and personal experience, the literature available and from experiences and feed-back in previous stress-management programmes.

Taking Care of Your Body

Regular aerobic-style exercise

Before embarking on any exercise programme, you should consult your doctor.

Aerobic-style exercise includes swimming, cycling, walking, jogging non-stop for at least twenty minutes every day or a minimum of three times a week. This form of exercise burns up the chemicals and hormones that are harmful to physical and emotional wellbeing. In addition, it appears to release chemicals and hormones that are analgesic and antidepressant.

I conducted research on the symptoms and treatment of depression and stress and found that in all cases regular exercise relieved symptoms, reduced stress and lifted depression.

Dr Smith, the stressed general practitioner, telephoned me a month after the stress-management programme that he had attended. He asked for an individual consultation. He told me he had encouraged his wife to play golf with him once a week. This gave them time with each other. A babysitter had been organised to look after the children. The marriage relationship was improving and the couple were planning a weekend away. In addition, he had joined their local gym where he spent one hour swimming, three times a week. He reported that his head was clearer and he was no longer irritable at work. He also felt more relaxed at home.

A healthy balanced diet

This is a diet rich in unrefined carbohydrates, fresh fruits and vegetables. Protein should be in the form of fish, pulses and poultry with less red meat and fat. For an individualised diet programme, a doctor or dietician should be consulted.

Dorothy Kussen, the widowed school teacher, wrote me a letter six months after she had attended our programme.

She stated that she had drastically cut down on fats and sugar and had lost twenty of the thirty extra kilograms she had been carrying. Her confidence had increased dramatically and she had recently met a kind, single man who she thought could be a lifetime companion. The children were still creating tension for her, but she was more assertive with them.

Moderate Alcohol Consumption and Ceasing Cigarette Smoking

Professional help or a professional programme can assist you in your efforts to reduce alcohol consumption or cease cigarette smoking.

Relaxation

This could be the deep-muscle relaxation taught in this programme, meditation, autohypnosis (learnt from a reputable hypnotherapist), or simply sitting in a peaceful place with time to experience peace of mind within and the beauty without.

A number of years ago, a young student consulted me for examination stress. She had been missing exams due to panic attacks, fear of failure, fainting and sweating. She learned the deep-muscle relaxation of this programme, visualising the liquid in her body as green. She taught this method to her fellow students who referred to me as 'the green slime'. This young student is now a successful professional, who reports that to this day she still uses the 'green slime' as an integral part of balancing her busy life with periods of relaxation.

Efficient Time Management

This is where the individual avoids workaholism, including 'hurry sickness'. It precludes procrastination and emphasises a lifestyle that is characterised by the allotment of time in a balanced way to hard work, hard play and periods of relaxation. Time management includes the use of a telephone answering machine when the telephone at home is a stressor and the delegation of tasks to others where this is possible.

This method involves regular list-making, on a daily or at least weekly basis, where demands and pressures are prioritised. These lists should include all tasks that need to be completed, both at work and at home. They should then be structured in order of importance or priority — number one being the most important and the last one being the least important. The tasks must be handled systematically, from the highest to the lowest priority. It often happens that the last (or last few) tasks on the list are unnecessary to complete at all. Once the most important tasks are completed, there is a feeling of relief, control and hence greater self-confidence.

Jane Harper, the stressed attorney mentioned earlier, made a commitment at the end of her workshop to purchase an answering machine. I telephoned her six weeks after the workshop to find out how she was coping. She said that the answering machine had materialised. It had been wonderful as it meant that family meals could be enjoyed without interruption. She also said that she had been exercising regularly and that she and her husband had planned and booked weekend breaks — some with and some without the children. She was feeling much happier. She had been using the relaxation tape once a week and had been unwinding for a few moments between each client.

Allotting Sufficient Time to Family and Friends

This leads to a sense of belonging, closeness and caring and is thus an essential stress manager.

Utilising Creativity

Utilise creativity, such as making art, playing a musical instrument, singing, acting, sewing, knitting, interior decorating, pottery or gardening. These express emotions that are deep-seated and thus release the stress of keeping these feelings suppressed.

Our stress-management programme utilises creativity as an integral balancing agent; clay modelling with music through which the participants introduce themselves to each other.

Creative visualisation is used with music. The importance of the healing potential of colour is emphasised — for example, greens, blues and pale greys are soothing, mauve is a healing colour whilst yellow is positive and strong. Shades of red depict anger and black, depression.

In addition to the above, we make collages at the end of the programme to describe what the participants have learnt and what they will take with them into the future. To this end we provide magazines, sheets of blank paper, crayons or felt-tip pens and scissors. The participants explain their collage to the group and thus learn from each other.

At one of our workshops, a participant would not leave once the others had gone and we were packing away. She confided that she could have continued all night.

She was a 49-year-old married woman who was experiencing problems in her marriage to a workaholic. She eventually left our workshop, went home and suggested to her husband that they each make a collage. She brought both his and her collages to me the following week. Of interest was the fact that she and her husband were predominantly left-brain thinkers. The introduction of creativity showed clearly that they wished for a more balanced relationship-oriented lifestyle where nature, colours, silence or gentle communication, touch and peace were integrated into their lives.

My area of creativity is chiefly painting on canvas. It does, however, include gourmet cooking, listening to music and interior design. I realised the importance of creativity as a medium for stress management when I met a couple who lectured at the University of Cape Town Michaelis School of Art.

They invited me to revisit this school, where I had survived a mere six months in Graphic Design after the completion of high school. The visit twenty years later was accompanied by an instruction to listen to wonderful music by Vivaldi, not to imagine that I would hang my completed painting on the wall, but just to enjoy myself.

The next five hours felt like a few minutes. I had emptied my soul onto the canvas and could see clearly where I was in terms of emotions at that particular time. Art has become a necessary passion in my life which, I believe, would be poorer without it.

Appreciating the Creativity of Others

Appreciate the creativity of others as in listening to music, enjoying good food, visiting art galleries or buildings of aesthetic value.

Taking Advantage of the Beauty of Nature

Take frequent short and long trips to the beach, into nature or into your own garden. This method tends to refresh and replenish the body and mind. There is thus a new release of energy for further constructive activity.

A matron of a psychiatric clinic described to one of our groups how she wakes up thirty minutes earlier than necessary each working day. She goes into her lush tropical garden and waters and feeds her plants or just listens to the sounds of silence and relaxes this way before a day guaranteed to be stressful. She stated that without nature (her garden) at the start of her day and exercise at the end of her day, she would need to book herself into her clinic as an in-patient.

Learning a New Language or Skill

When a person is suffering from the stress of boredom, it is helpful to introduce another stimulating activity. This seems to fulfil and satisfy, rather than further stress the individual. The person whose work involves service to others, for example, in medicine, psychology, social work, insurance brokering or law would benefit from a skill that focuses on a more solitary activity such as computer programming.

Physical and Emotional Intimacy

The skin is a person's largest sense organ. This programme promotes the view that sensual enrichment is an essential stress manager. It follows then that touching and the physical/sexual expression of feelings is effective in stress management. However, a physical relationship without emotional intimacy tends to leave the people involved only temporarily satisfied. With emotional closeness, there is a sense of a committed and secure base from which the individual can grow and learn, at home and at work.

Body Massage, Reflexology and Aromatherapy

Body massage, reflexology and aromatherapy are recommended, either in the absence of an intimate relationship, or as additional sensory stimulation. These treatments will fill one with a sense of pampering oneself that can only be seen as positive.

Financial Management

Expert financial managers, such as Noel Whitakker and Magnus Heystek*, propose that financial stress is one of the heaviest burdens that people face today. Larry Burkett** stresses that it is not how much or how little the people

---

*   Whittaker N. & Heystek M. *Making Money made Simple*
**   Burkett L. *Victory over Debt.*

earn, but rather how well or badly they manage to live within their means. It has been our experience that individuals who manage their finances effectively have a sense of coping, confidence and wellbeing.

Positive Thinking

Engender positive thinking in yourself and in those around you. Scott Peck* stated that life is tough and once a person acknowledges that life is difficult and fraught with crises, it becomes more manageable and less tough. Acceptance of life's crises is the first step towards positive thinking. It is quite normal to be anxious, distressed and even depressed at the cards one is dealt in life.

Allow yourself a limited period of self-pity, after which it becomes necessary, not only to identify the actual problem, but also to decide what action to take to effect change. It is also helpful to look for the positive lessons and growth that inevitably arise from life's crises.

Positive thinking includes a spiritual or religious belief system where one accepts that each person is sent certain lessons. Free choice involves deciding whether to face these tasks in a positive, constructive manner or whether to avoid life's difficulties and choose rather to be a victim, miserable, stressed and depressed.

Support Systems

Use your support systems both at work (colleagues) and at home (family and friends). We have been brought up to believe that healthy, well-adjusted people are those who cope independently with several demands and life pressures. We have been taught that it is a sign of weakness, especially for men, to cry and that one should not ask others for assistance, as this will burden colleagues, family and friends.

---

* Peck, S. *The Road Less Travelled.*

All of the above are misconceptions. Asking for colleagues' assistance is a part of healthy assertive behaviour — see section on assertiveness.

Men need to learn to express feelings, including joy and sorrow — this will relieve stress, reduce family violence and promote personal growth.

One, or a few trustworthy friends and family members could save your sanity because you can share deep pleasures and profound pain with them. The sharing is mutual — from you to them and *vice versa*. It is simply one's willingness to listen that promotes further closeness.

On occasion they or you may ask for practical assistance. This allows the other to feel prized and needed.

One of our participants 'phoned me after a workshop to report that, for the first time in her life, she had asked a neighbour to replace a rather tricky and high-up light bulb in her garden.

She was delighted at his positive response and at her courage in asking. She skipped and danced home from the neighbour's house.

Religious or Spiritual Support

A religious or spiritual belief system is essential to balance in a world that is based on conflicting values, including excessive material values. Scott Peck* talks of this belief system as GRACE. Hanson** discusses faith as an integral balancing element. Dale Carnegie*** writes of faith as an antidote to fear.

It has been my experience that individuals who have an insatiable hunger for affection and for material goods most often have little faith and trust in energy sources that are more powerful than the individual. Some people find

---

*   Peck, S. *The Road Less Travelled.*
**   Hanson, P. *The Joy of Stress.*
*** Carnegie, D. *How to Stop Worrying and Start Living.*

religious peace of mind in ritualised and regular attendance at church, synagogue or mosque services. Others seek and find 'soul food' in nature, either hiking up a mountain, watching the sea or simply enjoying the serenity of their own garden. Still others find spiritual or religious support through the expression of their creative talents.

I have an ongoing conversation with my Maker. I give thanks for assistance that I have been given from time to time, and ask for guidance and support in decision-making.

My religion is Judaism although I attend the synagogue on an irregular basis. This is a place where no telephones ring and where ancient prayers are chanted, as they have been over many centuries. Also, the traditional music soothes and heals my soul.

Assertiveness Training

Together with deep-muscle relaxation and the other stress managers examined above, assertive behaviour is an invaluable stress-management skill. Manuel Smith* describes assertiveness training in a concise and amusing manner. This section is based on his book.

It is also based on my research into the treatment of depression and anxiety.** Assertive behaviour is practising clear communication skills to deal effectively with manipulative conflict situations. These skills prevent aggression or withdrawal (the 'fight or flight' response).

We have all experienced the situation in which a stranger stands too close to us and invades our personal, psychological space. This evokes strong feelings regarding close proximity. These feelings are intuitive gut reactions to others invading our personal space.

From an early age, children are taught to ignore their first gut reaction or inner feelings to anything. This they do by

---

*   Smith, M. *When I Say No I Feel Guilty.*
**   Musikanth, S.J. 'Two Methods in the Treatment of Depression.'

clouding their feelings with explanations, defences and rationalisations about why the feelings are incorrect. These defences prevent clear, direct communication of feelings and needs to others. They also result in the doubting of the individual's ability to judge his/her feelings and subsequent actions. This process of self-doubt frequently results in lack of self-confidence, anxiety, periodic or persistent depression.

An excellent way in which we can suffer less anxiety, less depression or guilt is to hear and trust our own gut reactions. As we make choices that are right for ourselves we become more self-confident and in control.

Assertive behaviour may best be explained by means of Smith's* ten basic assertive rights.

1. You are the judge of your own behaviour and must take responsibility for its initiation and consequences.

2. You do not have to explain or excuse your own behaviour.

3. You are not responsible for other people's problems. You may, however, offer advice.

4. You may change your mind.

5. You have the right to make mistakes and to take responsibility for them.

6. You are at liberty to say 'I don't know'.

7. You do not have to please others in order to cope with them.

8. You have the right to be illogical in making a decision. This happens sometimes when you are making a decision based on gut feelings.

9. You have the right to say 'I don't understand' in the face of veiled criticism from those close to you.

10. You have the right to say 'I don't care', 'I don't want to' or simply 'NO' without feeling guilty.

*   Smith, M. *When I Say No I Feel Guilty*

To effectively assert yourself, it is necessary to know your assertive rights, to listen to your gut reactions and then to act assertively on these.

Refusing Unreasonable Requests

This is the first assertive skill of this programme. Think of a situation where someone at work or at home is demanding time or material gain from you. Your gut reaction to this request is loudly and clearly telling you to refuse.

The person is attempting to make you agree by inducing guilt feelings. In this situation, express understanding of the person's need and then say 'no' with no explanation, defence, aggression or withdrawal.

Coping with Criticism

The usual reaction to criticism is a feeling of anxiety. This is often accompanied by guilt. There are three responses — fogging, negative assertion and negative enquiry — that empower instead of making you feel guilt or anxiety. In each of these you do not deny the criticism, defend or explain. You also do not counterattack.

Fogging

Fogging, according to Smith,* is a response to manipulative criticism in formal or commercial situations. You respond to the criticism as if you were in a fog. The criticism is construed as a stone being thrown at the fog:

○ fog offers no resistance to the stone;
○ it does not retaliate;
○ the stone passes through the fog; and
○ inevitably people will give up trying to change the persistent, independent, non-manipulative fog and leave it alone.

---

*   Smith, M. *When I Say No I Feel Guilty.*

When you are criticised in formal or commercial situations:

- ○ do not deny the criticism;
- ○ do not become defensive or explain; and
- ○ do not counterattack.

RATHER:

Agree with any truth in statements the person uses to criticise you.

> For example: 'You should not smoke.'
>
> If you are a smoker respond with:
>
> 'You are correct, I should not smoke.'

Agree with any possible truth in critical statements. For example:

> 'All these years you have condoned the apartheid system by living in an affluent 'white' area and by employing a black domestic worker.'
>
> A further example: 'Your casual dress at work undermines your professionalism.'
>
> In both of these instances the person could be right (on a scale of probability from 0 to 100). You therefore respond with:
>
> 'You may be right,' 'You could be right,' 'Perhaps you are right.'

Agree with the general truth in logical, manipulative, critical statements.

> Your elderly mother says: 'Children should show consideration for their parents by including them in all social arrangements.'
>
> You respond with: 'You are right, children should consider their parents.'

From the above statements, it is clear that you are responding only to the truth, the possible truth or the general truth in the content of critical, manipulative statements levelled against you.

Listen carefully to what the person says, and remember that you are the final judge of your own behaviour. You are thus free to continue the criticised behaviour or to change it when you judge it to be wrong.

Negative Assertion

This skill enables you to cope assertively when faced with hostile criticism of your errors (Smith)*. Everyone makes mistakes from time to time. It is important not to respond with guilt or anxiety when your errors are criticised. Accept the fact that mistakes are mistakes, no more and no less.

When criticised for your errors:

- O agree with the truth, possible truth or general truth in the criticism;
- O apologise for your mistake; and
- O offer empathy for any inconvenience that you may have caused.

For example: 'You have shown gross irresponsibility and lack of respect by forgetting our appointment for lunch.'

You respond with: 'It was irresponsible of me not to note our appointment in my diary. I am sorry to have inconvenienced you. Next time I won't rely on my memory, but rather on my diary.'

Negative Inquiry and Negotiating Workable Compromise

Whilst fogging and negative assertion are useful in formal and commercial situations, they are aimed at people with whom you have no intention of developing closeness. They are passive skills. They do not encourage intimacy, understanding or non-manipulative interaction between spouses, partners, relatives or close friends.

---

* Smith, M. *When I Say No I Feel Guilty.*

In handling criticism from those you care about, it is more appropriate to use the assertive skill Smith* developed and termed negative inquiry.

As with fogging and negative assertion, you do not use:

○ denial;
○ defensiveness;
○ manipulative statements of right or wrong; or
○ blaming.

Rather break the manipulative cycle by actively encouraging further criticism about yourself and more information about the other person. This is achieved in a calm and unemotional manner. Do not use a sarcastic tone of voice.

This skill encourages the other person to:

○ state their needs and wants more assertively; and
○ ultimately promotes the finding of a workable compromise.

Respond to this type of criticism with requests for more information. For example:

'You always arrive home late when we have arrangements to go out alone for dinner.' You respond with: 'Now that you point it out to me, I think you are right. What is it about my coming late that bothers you?'

Your spouse/partner might respond with: 'You seem to make work your priority rather than me.'

or 'Maybe you find my company boring.'

or 'By the time you arrive home, my anticipation of spending a delightful evening with you is clouded with frustration and anger.'

You will find that with this type of inquiry you arrive at the crux of the person's dissatisfaction and may, in accordance

---

* Smith, M. *When I Say No I Feel Guilty.*

with your intuitive gut reaction, offer a workable compromise that will resolve the given conflict.

Remember, in assertive behaviour:

○ do not defend or explain yourself;
○ do not deny criticism;
○ do not become aggressive or withdrawn;
○ say what you want or do not want clearly and assertively;
○ respond to the content of the other person's request or criticism and not to the implication that you should feel guilty or anxious;
○ accept mistakes and admit to them; and
○ encourage those close to you to express themselves clearly and non-manipulatively.

This will engender further closeness and the possibility of a workable compromise when faced with conflict.

6

COMMITMENT TO A STRESS-MANAGEMENT TECHNIQUE

Having discussed a broad and varied spectrum of stress managers, it is important for you to look more carefully at these.

Choose one technique that you have thus far resisted including in your life.

Turn to a blank page in your notepad and head it:

Commitment

Write down the stress manager that you wish to commit to.

Write down:

○ why you think this technique is important to include in your life;

○ where you will regularly fit it into your life;

○ how you will make the time available to do so; and

○ which important person you are going to tell about this commitment.

CONCLUSION

This programme has examined stress, its effects on physical and emotional processes, its causes and management.

The aim has been to provide you with a repertoire of ideas and practical skills. We hope you will tailor these to positively harness the stressors in your life. We want you to balance these with regular intervals of rest and relaxation. This balancing skill will achieve a stimulating, challenging and healthy lifestyle.

We conclude this workshop by making a collage. You will need:

○ a sheet of plain paper;
○ old magazines;
○ scissors;
○ glue;
○ coloured pencils or felt-tipped pens; and
○ music.

Think about what you have learned on this programme and what you will take with you to use in your life.

Switch on the music.

Cut or tear pictures and words from the magazines. Do not try to be neat.

Paste these onto the paper.

You may draw or write whatever you like on or between the pasted pictures or words.

Look carefully at your collage and tell yourself or others what you have learned about your life through this programme.

Tell yourself — and preferably others — what you are going to use in your life.

RECOMMENDED READING

Alberti, R. & Emmons, M. 1975. *Stand up, Speak out, Talk back.* Pocket Books.

Alberti, R. & Emmons, M. 1990. *Your Perfect Right.* Impact.

Benson, H. 1975. *The Relaxation Response.* William Morrow.

Benson, H. 1984. *Beyond the Relaxation Response.* William Morrow.

Burkett, L. 1992. *Victory Over Debt.* Northfield.

Carnegie, D. 1984. *How to stop Worrying and Start Living.* Revised edition. Pocket Books.

Cooper, C. L. & Davidson, M. J. 1991. *The Stress Survivors.* Harper Collins.

Hambly, K. 1989. *Overcoming Tension.* Richard Clay.

Hanson, P. 1987. *The Joy of Stress.* Pan Books.

Hanson, P. 1990. *Stress for Success.* Pan Books.

Holmes & Rahe. 1967. 'Life Change Index'. *Journal of Psychosomatic Research*, Vol.2, pp. 213-218.

Looker, T. & Gregson, O. 1989. *Stresswise.* Hodder & Stoughton.

Musikanth, S. J. 1981. 'Two Methods in the Treatment of Depression.' Masters Dissertation. UNISA.

Musikanth, S. J. 1985. 'Client-centred Psychotherapy in the Treatment of Depression.' Doctoral Thesis. UNISA.

Peck, S. 1978. *The Road Less Travelled*. Arrow Books.

Slaby, A. E. 1991. *60 Ways to Make Stress Work for You*. Bantam.

Sheehy, G. 1976. *Passages*. E. P. Dutton.

Sheehy, G. 1981. *Pathfinders*. Bantam Books.

Smith, M. 1976. *When I Say No I Feel Guilty*. Bantam Books.

Trauer, T. 1990. *Coping with Stress*. Tafelberg.

Whittaker, N. & Heystek, M. 1990. *Making Money Made Simple*. Struik Timmins.

ORDER FORM

- I wish to purchase .... stress kit/s @ R109,00 each = R .....
- I wish to purchase .... relaxation cassettes @ R60,00 each
  = R .....

  TOTAL   R ......

Name:

Address: Postal Code:

Company: Position:

Tel No.:   Fax No.:

(Kindly place an X in the appropriate boxes)

Enclosed is my cheque ☐ postal order ☐ money order ☐
for R ....

(Cheques, postal orders or money orders to be made out to
Matters Inc)

Charge my Visa Card ☐   Master Card ☐

Card No. ⊡⊡⊡⊡⊡⊡⊡⊡⊡⊡⊡⊡⊡⊡⊡⊡ Expiry Date:

Signature

(Please allow six weeks for delivery.)

I am interested in receiving further information on your workshops for
myself ☐   my company/business/institute ☐

Please send this order form together with your payment to:
Matters Inc.
18 Corsair Crescent
Constantia 7800
Cape Town
South Africa

For further information, kindly write to the above address or
Fax us at (021) 930-5997.

ORDER FORM

- I wish to purchase _____ sheets kits at R102.00 each x R _____
- I wish to purchase _____ relaxation cassettes @ R60.00 each.

TOTAL R _____

Name _____

Address _____ Postal Code _____

Company _____

Tel no. _____ Fax _____

(Kindly place an X in the appropriate boxes)

Enclosed is my cheque [ ] postal order [ ] money order [ ]

(Cheques, postal orders or money orders to be made out to Barbara Inc)

Charge my Visa card [ ] Master Card [ ]

Card no [ ][ ][ ][ ][ ][ ][ ][ ][ ][ ][ ][ ] Expiry Date [ ][ ]

Signature _____

(Please allow six weeks for delivery)

I am interested in receiving further information on your workshops for
myself [ ] my company/organisation more [ ]

Please send this order form together with your payment to:

Barbara Inc.
19 Ocean Crescent
Edgemead 7400
Cape Town
South Africa

For further information, kindly write to the above address or
fax us at (021) 555 _____

NOTEPAD

NOTEPAD

NOTEPAD

NOTEPAD

NOTEPAD

NOTEPAD

NOTEPAD

NOTEPAD

NOTEPAD

NOTEPAD

NOTEPAD

NOTEPAD

NOTEPAD

NOTEPAD

NOTEPAD

NOTEPAD

NOTEPAD

NOTEPAD

NOTEPAD

NOTEPAD

NOTEPAD

NOTEPAD